See What We Eat!
A First Book of Healthy Eating

Scot Ritchie

Kids Can Press

To Stacey. Thank you, you're the best! — S.R.

Kids Can Press gratefully acknowledges the financial support of the Government of Ontario, through the Ontario Media Development Corporation; the Ontario Arts Council; the Canada Council for the Arts; and the Government of Canada, through the CBF, for our publishing activity.

Published in Canada and the U.S. by
Kids Can Press Ltd.
25 Dockside Drive, Toronto, ON M5A 0B5

Kids Can Press is a Corus Entertainment Inc. company

www.kidscanpress.com

The artwork in this book was rendered digitally. The text is set in Futura.

Edited by Stacey Roderick
Designed by Julia Naimska

Printed and bound in Malaysia, in 3/2017 by Tien Wah Press (Pte) Ltd.

CM 17 0 9 8 7 6 5 4 3 2 1

Library and Archives Canada Cataloguing in Publication

Ritchie, Scot, author, illustrator
    See what we eat! : a first book of healthy eating / Scot Ritchie.

ISBN 978-1-77138-618-0 (hardback)

    1. Food — Juvenile literature. 2. Nutrition — Juvenile literature. I. Title.

TX355.R58 2017   j641.3   C2016-906464-6

Contents

Farm Fresh

Our five friends are going apple picking on Yulee's aunt's farm. They'd like to make an apple crisp to take to the potluck dinner at the community center. Everyone in the neighborhood is bringing a special dish to share to celebrate the fall harvest, the time of year when crops are ready to be gathered.

Do you ever think about where your food comes from? Or how it gets to your table or lunch box? A lot of our food is grown or raised on farms.

Food for Everyone!

On the drive to the farm, the friends talk about last year's harvest celebration. "There were so many different kinds of food to try!" says Nick.

There *are* many different foods. What's your favorite? Food can be divided into nutritional groups, such as grains, vegetables, protein, dairy and fruits. Eating a variety of foods from each group every day gives you more energy to play and think, helps you grow and makes you healthier.

Good Grains

Before the apple picking begins, Aunt Sara shows the kids around. The first stop is the field where wheat and oats are planted.

"These grains grow best with lots of sun," says Aunt Sara. Grains are loaded with fiber, vitamins and minerals. You get the most out of your grains by eating the whole kernel, or seed, such as in whole wheat bread, tortillas and chapatis or the oats in oatmeal.

Vegetable Rainbow

Next stop, the vegetable garden! Nick is surprised to see so many different vegetables. Beets and carrots grow below the ground but other vegetables, such as zucchini and green beans, grow above the ground.

A tasty way to get lots of different nutrients — what your body needs to grow and to stay healthy — is to eat a colorful assortment of vegetables.

Mmm, what a delicious-looking garden! But where are Yulee and Max running off to?

Protein Power

At the chicken coop, Aunt Sara shows Sally and Pedro how to carefully collect the freshly laid eggs. Later, the eggs will be cleaned and checked before they are sold.

Eggs are a great source of protein — and one of Yulee's favorite foods. She is excited to take some home so her dad can make his famous cheese-and-tomato omelet.

Pedro has an egg allergy and will get sick if he eats them. But he knows there are lots of other delicious foods that are safe for him to eat and are also good sources of protein, such as nuts, fish, meat, tofu and beans.

Delicious Dairy

Now the friends have arrived at the dairy where the cows and goats are milked. Before the milk is sold, it will be pasteurized, or heated to a high temperature, to get rid of harmful germs.

Milk is used to make other foods, such as butter, cheese, yogurt and ice cream. There are lots of nutrients in milk, including calcium, which helps you grow strong bones and teeth. Luckily for Nick, his favorite drink is a glass of cold milk. Yum!

Martin checks the apple crisp recipe and sees that it calls for butter. They will buy some at the store along with the other ingredients.

A Is for Apple

The friends have arrived at the orchard. It's time to pick some apples!

Aunt Sara knows when the apples are ready to be picked by counting the days from when the trees first bloomed. She can also tell when the fruit is ripe by its color, smell and taste.

"Start picking from the outside of the tree. Those apples are the ripest. And remember, twisting the apple off the branch makes it easier!" says Aunt Sara. Everybody joins in, and soon the baskets are full.

Fruit, such as these apples, is a sweet treat that's loaded with vitamins and minerals.

Get Your Energy!

Whew! Picking apples is hard work. Everyone is feeling a little tired and hungry, so it's time to rest and refuel!

Aunt Sara and the gang enjoy their snack of whole wheat crackers, cheese, hummus and carrots. Apples, too, of course! The friends know that making nutritious food choices gives you lots of energy.

They also make sure to drink water. Your body needs food and water to work well.

Ollie and Max need to refuel, too. Pedro makes sure they also get some food and water.

Food from around the World

It's time to go home and start baking, so everyone gets back in the van.

On the way, they drive past a large food warehouse. Foods that aren't grown or made locally are sent by truck, plane, train or ship and stored here.

Food from the warehouse is delivered to grocery stores to be sold.

Time to Shop

The gang has all the apples they need, but they have to stop at the grocery store for the other ingredients.

Martin finds the aisle with the oats and flour. Nick and Sally collect everything else: butter, brown sugar, nutmeg and cinnamon. While Aunt Sara is paying for the groceries, Pedro notices something — eggs from Valley Farms!

Food produced locally, such as the apples and eggs from Aunt Sara's farm, can be sent straight to nearby grocery stores or farmers' markets. That's fresh!

Let's Bake!

Pedro's dad has offered to help the friends make their dessert.

Before they begin, everyone washes their hands well with soap and water. Next the apples are washed.

Pedro's dad begins by peeling and cutting up the apples. Sally and Yulee measure out all the ingredients.

Nick and Martin follow the recipe directions. What a mess!

Mmm, I'm getting hungry again!

Compost the Most

While the apple crisp is baking, Yulee and Pedro run out to the backyard to put the apple peels in the compost bin.

Compost is organic food waste, such as fruit peels and eggshells, that has been allowed to decompose, or break down, naturally. It can be mixed into soil to help new plants grow.

Composting food scraps is another way of recycling. Pedro's dad mixes the compost into his garden soil to help the plants grow.

A Harvest Celebration

Mmm, the apple crisp smells great! Once it has cooled, the friends take it to the community center for the potluck.

Yulee puts the dish next to Mrs. Martinez's tamales and Mr. Gorski's cheese-and-potato pierogies.

Time to eat! Who do you like to share a meal with?

The table is filled with so many delicious dishes. What a wonderful way to celebrate the harvest!

Harvest Apple Crisp

This recipe makes about 8 servings. You will need a 9 x 13 inch (22 x 33 cm) baking dish; a peeler; a small, sharp knife; a medium-size mixing bowl; and measuring spoons and cups.

IMPORTANT: Have an adult help you with this recipe. An adult should always be in charge of the stove and any cutting.

Ingredients

8 apples, peeled, cored and sliced
1½ cups (375 mL) brown sugar
1 cup (250 mL) flour
1 cup (250 mL) oats
1 teaspoon (5 mL) cinnamon
1 teaspoon (5 mL) nutmeg
½ cup (125 mL) cold butter, cut into pieces

1. Heat oven to 375 degrees Fahrenheit (190 degrees Celsius).

2. Lightly coat the baking dish with butter or use a non-stick spray.

3. Layer the apple slices evenly over the bottom of the baking dish.

4. Mix the dry ingredients (brown sugar, flour, oats, cinnamon and nutmeg) together in the mixing bowl.

5. Rub the pieces of butter and dry ingredients together between your fingers until the mixture looks like crumbs.

6. Sprinkle the mixture over the apples.

7. Bake for about 30 minutes, until the topping is lightly browned.

8. Remove and let the crisp cool before serving.

9. Enjoy!

Words to Know

allergy: when a person's immune system reacts to something he or she has eaten, touched or breathed in as though it were harmful. A person having an allergic reaction may break out into a rash or hives, feel nauseated or have trouble breathing. It's important to know if someone has a food allergy before sharing your food. There are many foods people can be allergic to, including peanuts, fish and wheat.

calcium: a mineral found in dairy foods but also in other foods, such as leafy green vegetables, almonds and sardines. Calcium helps keep bones and teeth growing and strong.

carbohydrate: a nutrient that gives your body energy

dairy: the food group that includes milk and foods made with cow, sheep and goat milk. Many people replace dairy with foods made from soy milk, coconut milk, almond milk or rice milk.

fiber: a carbohydrate that comes from the plants we eat. Fiber helps food move through your digestive system.

fruit: the part of the plant that contains the seed and most of the nutrients. We usually eat the part of the fruit that grows around the seed.

grain: plants such as wheat and oats that provide you with proteins, vitamins, minerals, carbohydrates and fiber

nutrient: a substance in food that provides energy and helps your body grow and work well

pasteurize: the process of heating a liquid, such as milk, to a high enough temperature to kill germs

protein: a nutrient in food that protects your immune system and helps build muscles and organs

vegetable: the leaf, root or stem of a plant that you can eat. Vegetables are a good source of fiber and vitamins.